I0469107

The Impact of the Federal Estate Tax on State Estate Taxes

Steven Maguire
Specialist in Public Finance

October 24, 2012

Congressional Research Service

7-5700

www.crs.gov

R42788

CRS Report for Congress ———————————————————
Prepared for Members and Committees of Congress

Summary

An estate tax is a tax levied on the assets left behind by a decedent. The federal government and many state governments levy estate taxes or some type of tax on the transfer of assets at death. In 2012, the federal estate tax allows for a $5.12 million exclusion and a top rate of 35%. The federal estate tax is scheduled to revert to the pre-2001 structure on January 1, 2013, with a $1 million exclusion and top rate of 55%. The Administration's FY2013 budget proposes a federal estate tax with a $3.5 million exemption and top rate of 45% for 2013. Many states also levy estate or inheritance taxes (or both) that are linked to federal law. If the federal estate tax is allowed to revert to pre-2001 law, state and federal estate tax revenue will increase significantly by imposing a greater tax burden on estates than would an extension of 2012 law or the President's FY2013 budget proposal. The percentage increase in state estate tax revenue would likely be greater than the percentage increase in federal estate taxes under a return to pre-2001 law. The principal cause is the return of the federal credit for state death taxes when the tax changes originally enacted by the Economic Growth Tax Relief and Reconciliation Act in 2001 (EGTRRA, P.L. 107-16) expire.

Before EGTRRA, all 50 states and the District of Columbia imposed an estate tax where state estate taxes were linked directly to the federal credit for state death taxes paid ("death" taxes because the credit could also be used for inheritance and succession taxes). The dollar-for-dollar credit meant that state taxes were not an additional burden, creating the equivalent of a revenue sharing arrangement between the federal government and the states as most states structured their taxes to match exactly the federal credit. EGTRRA gradually replaced the federal credit with a deduction. Because of this change to a deduction, state estate and inheritance taxes were no longer offset on a dollar-for-dollar basis and, as a result, imposed an additional burden on estates and heirs. States were then lobbied for relief from this additional estate tax burden. As a result, by 2012, just 16 states and the District of Columbia imposed an estate tax and 8 states imposed an inheritance tax (2 states levied both).

As Congress considers the future of the federal estate tax, questions concerning the coordination of the tax with the states have arisen. This report examines the interaction of federal and state estate taxes under three policy alternatives: (1) extend the 2012 law, (2) revert to the pre-2001 law, and (3) return to the 2009 law as proposed in the Administration's FY2013 budget proposal. A fourth option, repeal of the federal estate tax, has also been proposed. If the federal estate tax were repealed, repeal of most remaining state estate taxes would likely follow. This option, however, would most likely be considered in the context of broader tax reform and is beyond the scope of this report.

Which course of action Congress will choose is uncertain and the impact on the states is unclear. What is more certain is that coordination with states would likely reduce administrative and compliance costs of the estate tax, increase the progressivity of the code generally, and possibly increase the economic efficiency of state estate taxes.

This report will be updated as legislative events warrant.

Contents

Figures

Tables

Contacts

Introduction

An estate tax is a tax levied on the assets left behind by a decedent. The federal government and many state governments levy estate taxes or some type of tax on the transfer of assets at death. Under current law, the estate tax is scheduled to revert to the pre-2001 structure on January 1, 2013, with a $1 million exemption and top rate of 55%. In contrast, the federal estate tax currently allows for a significantly higher exemption amount, $5.12 million, and a significantly lower top rate of 35%. With this as backdrop, it is believed that Congress is likely to act on the federal estate tax in the near term.

How Congress chooses to act will impact state governments. The Administration's FY2013 budget proposes a middle ground between those options with a $3.5 million exemption and top rate of 45%.[1] There is an important difference between these proposals: the 2012 law and the Administration's proposal each allow a *deduction* for state death taxes whereas the pre-2001 law provides a *credit* for those taxes.

For example, when an estate files a federal return for a death occurring in 2012, state estate taxes paid are deducted from the value of the estate before calculating tax liability. In contrast, under the pre-2001 law, the estate would calculate the federal estate tax liability then reduce the federal tax payment dollar-for-dollar for any state estate taxes paid.

Changes to the federal estate tax are in part responsible for a decline in state estate tax revenue from $9.07 billion in 2001 to $4.65 billion in 2009. If current law is extended or if the President's proposal enacted, then the recent trend of declining state estate tax revenues will likely continue (see **Figure 1**).

The interaction between federal and state tax policy, if not the estate tax explicitly, has drawn the interest of Congress. A recent congressional hearing, couched in discussions of potential tax reform, hinted at bipartisan interest in encouraging greater tax coordination between the federal government and the states (and among the states).[2] Senator Baucus, in his opening statement for the hearing, noted the following:

> We need to make sure our federal, state and local tax systems are working together. As part of tax reform, we should ask how we can help states collect taxes owed and how we can encourage standard rules to protect taxpayers from multiple taxes and needless complexity.[3]

Senator Hatch also acknowledged the potential impact of the tax interdependence between the different levels of government. His interest, however, was from a constitutional perspective:

---

[1] For more on current law, see CRS Report 95-416, *Federal Estate, Gift, and Generation-Skipping Taxes: A Description of Current Law*, by John R. Luckey.

[2] U.S. Congress, Senate Committee on Finance, *Tax Reform: What It Means for State and Local Tax and Fiscal Policy*, 112th Cong., 2nd sess., April 25, 2012.

[3] Sen. Max Baucus, "Hearing Statement of Senator Max Baucus Regarding Tax Reform and State and Local Tax and Fiscal Policy," April 25, 2012.

> Issues involving the federal impact on state and local revenues impact both the Constitution's separation of powers between the federal and state governments and the separate identity of the sovereign states.[4]

The bipartisan recognition that state taxes are affected by changes to federal tax law does not imply that there is agreement on how to structure the federal estate tax in 2013 and beyond. In the 112th Congress, S. 3412, The Middle Class Tax Cut Act, would allow the estate tax law to revert to the pre-2001 law. Alternatively, The Tax Hike Prevention Act of 2012 (S. 3413) and its companion, The Job Protection and Recession Prevention Act of 2012 (H.R. 8), would extend the 2012 estate tax parameters through 2013.

In general, the pre-2001 structure of the estate tax would tax significantly more estates than would the FY2013 budget proposal or extension of 2012 law.[5] Reversion to the pre-2001 structure would result in an estimated significantly more taxable estates in 2013 compared to the number of taxable returns filed in 2009 (**Table 1**).[6] The President's FY2013 budget proposal would tax fewer estates in 2013 than in 2009.[7] In absolute terms, the percentage of estates that are taxable under all proposals is relatively small, as roughly 2.4 million individuals over the age of 24 died in 2010.[8]

If Congress elects to maintain a federal estate tax, the impact on states will depend critically on the treatment of state death taxes.[9] Most critically, the impact will depend on the choice of whether to allow the state death tax to "count" against federal estate taxes and, if so, how. Other components, such as the exclusion amount, the top rate, and the valuation of transferred assets, will also be important. These factors, however, are less important from an intergovernmental coordination perspective with the possible exception of the exclusion amount—many states use the federal exclusion amount as the threshold for filing a state return.

This report provides an overview of the federal estate tax since 2001, highlighting recent trends in federal and state estate tax revenue. The report also analyzes the impact of the three policy options cited above, and presents an economic perspective of the policy options. The report will be updated as legislative events warrant.

---

[4] Sen. Orrin Hatch, "Hatch Statement at Finance Committee Hearing Examining the Impact of Tax Reform on State and Local Governments," April 25, 2012.

[5] For 2012, under the Tax Relief, Unemployment Insurance Reauthorization, and Jobs Creation Act of 2010 (TRUIRJCA), the top rate was set at 35%, the exemption amount set at $5 million, and the deduction for state death taxes was extended.

[6] Estimates are courtesy of: Urban-Brookings Tax Policy Center, "Table T11-0156: Estate Tax Returns and Liability Under Current Law and Various Reform Proposals, 2011-2021," June 2, 2011, available at http://www.taxpolicycenter.org/numbers/displayatab.cfm?Docid=3037&DocTypeID=7. The 2009 data are from the IRS and is the last filing year without a significant impact from the 2010 repeal.

[7] Urban-Brookings Tax Policy Center, "Table T11-0156: Estate Tax Returns and Liability Under Current Law and Various Reform Proposals, 2011-2021," June 2, 2011.

[8] U.S. Centers for Disease Control, Sherry L. Murphy, B.S.; Jiaquan Xu, M.D.; and Kenneth D. Kochanek, M.A., *National Vital Statistics Reports, Vol. 60, No. 4*, January 11, 2012. The report can be found here: http://www.cdc.gov/nchs/data/nvsr/nvsr60/nvsr60_04.pdf.

[9] As different states structure their taxes due at death differently—some tax the estate while others tax the recipient of an inheritance—this report refers to these taxes collectively as death taxes as does the federal tax code (26 U.S.C. § 2011).

Federal Estate Taxes: 2001 to 2012

As noted above, the federal estate tax will likely be an issue for Congress in the near term. Three alternatives are examined for this report: (1) revert to the pre-2001 law, (2) extend the 2012 law, and (3) return to the 2009 law as proposed in the Administration's FY2013 budget proposal (see **Table 1** for a summary of the proposals). Though there are many other options that could be considered, these three plans are receiving the most attention, and they broadly represent the trade-offs under current consideration. For example, the federal estate tax could be repealed. If the federal estate tax were repealed, repeal of state estate taxes would likely follow. This option would most likely be considered in the context of broader tax reform and is beyond the scope of this report. The following is an overview of the modifications to the estate tax since 2001.

The Pre-2001 Law

If the estate tax reverts to pre-2001 law in 2013 as scheduled, significantly more estates will be subject to tax. The pre-2001 law includes a $1 million exemption amount, a top rate of 55% (with a 5% surtax on estates valued between $10 million and $17.184 million), no spousal exemption portability, and a credit for state death taxes paid. The pre-2001 law would yield an estimated 52,500 taxable returns in 2013.

Table 1. Three Options for the Federal Estate Tax

For the 2013 Tax Year

Structural Parameter	Pre-2001 Law (Congressional Inaction)	Current Law (Extend 2012 Law)	2009 Law Extended (President's FY2013 Budget Proposal)
Exemption Amount	$1 million	$5.120 million	$3.5 million
Top Rate*	55%, plus 5% surtax on estates between $10 million and $17.184 million	35%	45%
State Estate Tax Treatment	Credit	Deduction	Deduction
Surviving Spouse Portability	no	yes	yes
Estimated Returns	52,500	4,000	7,000
Revenue Loss (in millions)	0	$31,207	$22,146

Source: The revenue loss estimate from the Joint Committee on Taxation, Table 12-2 116 (extend the 2012 law, S. 3413) and Table 12-2 112R1 (revert to 2009 law, S. 3412).

Notes: *The federal estate tax has several graduated rate brackets. See **Table 5** for the rate schedule.

The Economic Growth and Tax Relief Reconciliation Act of 2001

As noted above, the federal estate tax is scheduled to revert to the pre-2001 structure absent congressional action.[10] The changes are the result of the delayed sunset of the modifications

---

[10] For more on the federal estate tax, see CRS Report RL30600, *Estate and Gift Taxes: Economic Issues*, by Donald J. Marples and Jane G. Gravelle.

originally implemented by the Economic Growth and Tax Relief Reconciliation Act of 2001 (EGTRRA, P.L. 107-16). Under that law, several important estate tax parameters were changed to reduce the burden of the federal estate tax and eventually repeal the tax in 2010. The changes in the years leading up to expiration included gradually increasing the exemption amount (technically the unified credit exemption equivalent amount) from $1 million to $3.5 million in 2009, decreasing the top rate from 55% to 45% by 2009, and changing the credit for state death taxes to a deduction.[11] This final change fundamentally changed the relationship between state and federal estate taxes and led to a decline in both federal and state revenues generated by the estate tax.

Example: Value of a Credit for State Estate Taxes Paid vs. a Deduction

Following is an example of a hypothetical estate in Delaware valued at $7 million.[12] This example will use 2012 law except for the treatment of state death taxes paid ("death" taxes because the credit could also be used for inheritance and succession taxes).[13] In both scenarios, $92,640 in state death taxes are paid to Delaware. In scenario A, state death taxes paid to Delaware are credited dollar-for-dollar toward federal estate tax liability (pre-2001 law structure). In scenario B (current law), state death taxes paid to Delaware are allowed as a federal deduction. All other parameters are the same for each scenario and reflect 2012 law including the 35% top rate and $5.12 million exclusion. With scenario B, each dollar paid to Delaware reduces federal liability by $0.35, the marginal federal estate tax rate. In contrast, with scenario A, each dollar paid to Delaware reduces federal liability by one dollar (see **Table 2**).

Table 2. Federal Credit for State Estate Taxes vs. Deduction

Hypothetical $7 million Estate in Delaware in 2012

Estate Tax Calculation	(A) With Federal Credit	(B) With Federal Deduction
Value of Estate	$7,000,000	$7,000,000
Federal Deduction for Delaware Estate Tax Paid	n/a	$92,640
Taxable Estate	$7,000,000	$6,907,360
Tentative Federal Tax Liability*	$2,430,800	$2,398,376
Tax Credits		
Equivalent Exemption (for $5.12 Million)	$1,772,800	$1,772,800
Delaware Estate Taxes Paid	$92,640	n/a
Final Federal Tax Liability	$565,360	$625,576
Grand Total: Federal and State Taxes	$658,000	$718,216
Effective Federal Tax Rate	8.1%	8.9%
Difference in dollars	n/a	$60,216

---

[11] The estate tax exemption is not structured like exemptions in the individual income tax. For the estate tax, a credit is offered for the taxes that would have been due on the amount of the exemption amount. Thus, for 2012, the exemption amount is $5.12 million and the credit for the $5.12 million of estate asset value is $1,772,800.

[12] Delaware is scheduled to repeal their estate tax on January 1, 2013.

[13] There are a significant number of additional assumptions to simplify the example such as no deductions for spouses or charities. It is also important to note that very few estates in any given year are valued at $7 million or more.

Source: CRS calculations.

Notes: *The tax tables used to calculate the federal and state tax liabilities are reproduced in **Table 5** and **Table 6**.

Under current 2012 law with a deduction for state estate taxes, the estate pays $60,216 more in federal taxes when compared to a credit method, but the state liability remains the same, $92,640. The liability is higher because only 35% of the estate tax paid to Delaware offsets federal liability. If the credit for state death taxes were to replace the deduction (scenario "A"), Delaware's estate tax would not change the total liability as long as the tax were structured to "pick-up" the federal credit. Thus, with the deduction structure, total estate taxes paid is greater than under the credit method.

Changes in Federal and State Estate Tax Revenue 2001 to 2009

The changes implemented by EGTRRA have had and will have a significant impact on both federal and state tax revenues on transfers at death. Combined federal and state revenue from estate and inheritance taxes has declined from $31.0 billion in 2001 ($37.5 billion in 2009 dollars) to $25.3 billion in 2009 (see **Figure 1**).[14] The decline, however, was much more significant for states: a 48% drop for state taxes compared to a 27% drop for the federal tax. Reversion to pre-2001 law would likely reverse this revenue change, increasing state estate tax revenue more rapidly than federal estate tax revenue.

The impact of federal changes to the estate tax on the states arises for a variety of reasons. First, most state estate taxes are linked directly or indirectly to the federal estate tax law. So, for example, when the federal exemption increased the filing threshold, states that were coupled with the federal law *as currently in place* saw their filing thresholds increase automatically. States had the option of proactively changing their laws, such as decoupling from the federal law, to maintain their estate tax revenue. Most states, however, did not change their laws for administrative or political reasons.

---

[14] Data for 2010 and 2011 are available, but are affected by the repeal of the federal estate tax in 2010 and do not provide a good basis for assessing the interaction between federal and state taxes on transfers at death going forward. Clearly, the repeal had an effect. For the 2010 tax year, the federal estate tax generated $13.2 billion, likely from deaths occurring before 2010. State collections were $3.9 billion in FY2010 and $4.5 billion in FY2011. Thus, the decline from 2001 accelerated through 2010 with combined collections of $17.1 billion. The FY2011 state tax data, which includes the first six months of 2011, spikes as the federal estate tax returned for 2011. U.S. Bureau of the Census, *State Government Tax Collections: 2011*, available at http://www.census.gov/govs/statetax/.

Figure 1. Federal and State Estate Tax Revenue, by Filing Year

Amounts are in '000s of 2009 Dollars

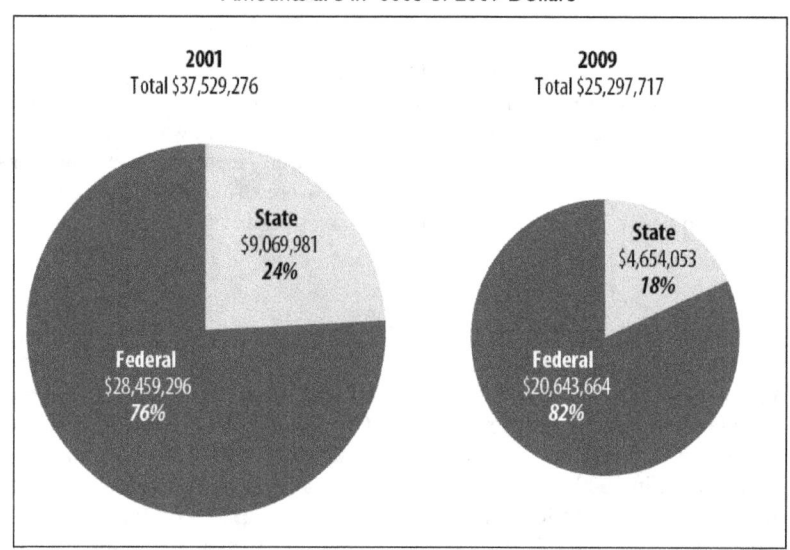

Source: Federal data are from the Internal Revenue Service and the state data are from the U.S. Census Bureau.

Second, EGTRRA changed the credit for state death taxes to a deduction beginning with the 2005 tax year. The impact on state estate tax revenue and structure was significant. The dollar-for-dollar federal credit for state death taxes meant that the state estate tax did not add any additional estate tax burden, as it offset some part of federal liability. The change to the deduction under EGTRRA meant that state estate taxes would impose an additional burden on decedent estates. This led to pressure, at the state level, to change state death taxes after passage of EGTRRA— something many states (26 states and the District of Columbia) have done.[15]

The 2012 Estate Tax

The Tax Relief, Unemployment Insurance Reauthorization, and Job Creation Act of 2010 (TRUIRJCA, P.L. 111-312; 124 Stat. 3296) reinstated the expired estate tax retroactively for 2010 and extended it through 2012. Under TRUIRJCA, the top rate is set at 35% (the top individual income tax rate) and the exemption set at $5 million (adjusted for inflation thereafter). TRUIRJCA also extended the deduction for state estate taxes through 2012 and continued the portability of any unused spousal exemption (effectively doubling the exemption for married decedents). Through the remainder of 2012, the exemption is set at $5.12 million. If Congress extends the 2012 law through 2013 (with the parameters indexed for inflation), an estimated 4,000 estates would be taxable in 2013.[16]

---

[15] The changes vary significantly by state. McGuireWoods LLP provides periodic updates of the current state of state death taxes. The most recent update was July 7, 2012: http://www.mcguirewoods.com/news-resources/publications/taxation/state_death_tax_chart.pdf.

[16] Estimates are from the Urban-Brookings Tax Policy Center, Table "T11-0156 - Baseline Estate Tax Returns; Current Law and Multiple Reform Proposals," 2011-2021, June 2, 2011. The table is available at http://www.taxpolicycenter.org/numbers/displayatab.cfm?Docid=3037&DocTypeID=7.

The President's FY2013 Budget Proposal

The President's FY2013 budget proposes returning the federal estate tax to the 2009 parameters on a permanent basis. Under the President's proposal, the top rate would be 45% and the exclusion amount $3.5 million for the federal estate tax.[17] The portability of the spousal exclusion would also be made permanent. When measured against current law, this proposal would generate a revenue loss of $312.3 billion over the 10-year budget window when compared to current law (pre-2001 law). The President's proposal would yield an estimated 7,000 taxable returns in 2013.[18]

Other Taxes

There are two related taxes the federal government levies at death: gift taxes and generation-skipping taxes. The estate tax is a tax on the wealth holdings of a decedent and is collected before assets are transferred to heirs. In contrast, gift taxes, which are often linked to an estate tax to stem tax avoidance strategies such as giving away assets at the end of life to skirt the estate tax, are not incurred at death. The federal gift tax has been "unified" with the estate tax in the past, meaning any taxable gifts during a lifetime were counted against any credits for federal estate taxes. The estate and gift taxes are not unified for the 2012 tax year and instead have separate exclusion amounts.

Generation-skipping transfer taxes (GSTs) are also intended to blunt tax planning strategies designed to avoid taxes. Generally, a generation-skipping transfer is a transfer to a grandchild (or great-grandchild) usually through a trust (a fund or account where the grandchild is the beneficiary). The transfer is taxable for the gift-giver at the highest rate of the estate tax at the time of transfer. The estate tax exemption amount, however, can be used to offset any GST tax. These taxes are an administrative patch to the estate tax intended to prevent aggressive tax planning utilizing a more distant decedent. For the remainder of this report, GSTs will not be directly addressed.

The tax on capital gains is another important element of the tax structure on assets transferred at death. Generally, capital gains are taxable when the gains are realized. Estates often have considerable unrealized capital gains included in the estate.[19] Without an estate tax, a significant amount of income would escape taxation. The estate tax, in a sense, replaces capital gains taxes or is intended to capture these unrealized gains.[20] Generally, once the asset is transferred, the value of the asset (or the basis) for the recipient is the market value on the date of the decedent's death ("stepped up" basis). Thus, any unrealized gains by the decedent are left untaxed. An alternative valuation method, the carry-over basis, has the heir assume the basis of the decedent (sometimes referred to as "stepping into the shoes" of the decedent). Any unrealized gain transferred to the heir would be taxable once the heir sold the asset. All of the proposals identified in this report follow the step-up in value of assets (the basis) transferred at death.

---

[17] The gift tax would not be unified with the estate tax and would have separate $1 million exclusion.

[18] Ibid.

[19] James M. Poterba and Scott Weisbenner, "The Distributional Burden of Taxing Estates and Unrealized Capital Gains at the Time of Death," in *Rethinking Estate and Gift Taxation,* William G. Gale, James R. Hines Jr., and Joel Slemrod Eds., Brookings Institution Press, 2001.

[20] For more on capital gains taxes, see CRS Report 96-769, *Capital Gains Taxes: An Overview,* by Jane G. Gravelle.

State Estate, Inheritance, and Gift Taxes in 2012[21]

The impact of the impending changes will vary across states. As of 2012, 22 states and DC imposed some type of tax on transfers at death (see **Table 3**).[22] Two states, Delaware and Ohio, are scheduled to repeal their estate taxes in 2013: Delaware on January 1, 2013, and Ohio on July 1, 2013.[23] A recent report by the Minnesota House Research Department identified 14 states (and DC) with an estate tax, 6 states with an inheritance tax, 2 states with both an estate tax and an inheritance tax, and 2 with a stand-alone gift tax.[24]

Generally, states with an estate tax use the now expired (but scheduled to return for the 2013 calendar year) rate schedule used to calculate the federal credit for state death taxes.[25] The incorporation of the federal tax code can be automatic, meaning if the credit for state death taxes were to return in the federal tax code, the state estate tax would also return.[26] Or, the link to the federal tax code can be as of a specific date, such as January 1, 2009. Three states, Connecticut, Ohio, and Washington, have completely independent estate taxes.[27] For the "decoupled" state estate taxes, state legislative action may be required to reinstate an estate tax.

The initial exemption amount varies among states, ranging from $338,333 in Ohio to $5 million in North Carolina. Seven states use a $1 million exemption. Fourteen states and the District of Columbia follow the federal state death tax credit with a graduated rate schedule that reaches 16% for estates valued over $10.1 million. Washington State levies a top rate of 19% and Ohio a much lower 7%.

State inheritance taxes are less common than estate taxes. These taxes, levied on heirs rather than the estate, are more analogous to income taxes. Differential exemption amounts and tax rates based on relation to the decedent are common at the state level. Eight states levy a tax on heirs and four states allow a complete exemption for lineal heirs.[28] The exemption amounts in the remaining states range from $3,500 (Pennsylvania) to $1 million (Tennessee).[29]

---

[21] This section of the report relies primarily on the research presented by Minnesota House of Representatives: Michael, Joel, "Survey of State Estate, Inheritance, and Gift Taxes," Minnesota House of Representatives Research Department, *Information Brief*, updated November 2011. The reported will be abbreviated as MHR.

[22] Minnesota House of Representatives Research Department, *Survey of State Estate, Inheritance, and Gift Taxes*, November 2011, p. 2.

[23] The three taxes typically identified as transfer taxes at death at the state level are estate taxes, inheritance taxes, and gift taxes. The gift tax is applicable to transfers between living individuals (called inter-vivos) and is intended to stem estate tax avoidance strategies such as end-of-life giving.

[24] Minnesota House of Representatives Research Department, *Survey of State Estate, Inheritance, and Gift Taxes*, November 2011, p. 2.

[25] 26 U.S.C. § 2011.

[26] According to the McGuireWoods LLP pamphlet cited earlier, 30 states are tied directly to the federal credit as of July 2012.

[27] The Ohio estate tax is scheduled for repeal beginning in 2013.

[28] A lineal heir would be immediate family and grandchildren, but the definition varies by state.

[29] Minnesota House of Representatives Research Department, *Survey of State Estate, Inheritance, and Gift Taxes*, November 2011, p. 9.

Table 3. State Estate, Inheritance, and Gift Taxes for 2011 Decedents

State	Estate	Inheritance	Gift
Total	17	8	2
Connecticut	x		x
Delaware	x		
District of Columbia	x		
Hawaii	x		
Illinois	x		
Indiana		x	
Iowa		x	
Kentucky		x	
Maine	x		
Maryland	x	x	
Massachusetts	x		
Minnesota	x		
Nebraska		x	
New Jersey	x	x	
New York	x		
North Carolina	x		
Ohio	x		
Oregon	x		
Pennsylvania		x	
Rhode Island	x		
Tennessee		x	x
Vermont	x		
Washington	x		

Source: CRS presentation of data reported in Minnesota House of Representatives Research Department, *Survey of State Estate, Inheritance, and Gift Taxes,* November 2011, p. 2.

Federal and State Estate Taxes: An Economic Analysis

Tax policy economists commonly evaluate a tax on four criteria: (1) administrative simplicity and compliance cost, (2) equity, (3) economic efficiency, and (4) revenue sufficiency. Following is an analysis of the changes to the estate tax since 2001 using these four criteria. Consideration of these criteria may help Congress as deliberations over the estate tax and tax reform are likely to continue in the coming months.

Administrative Simplicity and Compliance Cost

The administrative simplicity and compliance cost of a tax is important to revenue collectors and taxpayers. Revenue collectors prefer taxes that are easily administered and taxpayers prefer taxes where compliance is relatively easy. These factors are even more critical for taxes that are levied by different levels of government on a shared base like estate taxes. Intergovernmental coordination can improve both administrative simplicity and compliance costs.

There are two directions of coordination for taxes on a common base: "vertical" coordination and "horizontal" coordination.[30] Vertical coordination is between the federal government and the states and horizontal coordination is among the states. The level of vertical coordination between federal and state estate taxes has eroded significantly since the 2001 changes. As of 2012, many states have abandoned the estate tax completely while others have decoupled from the federal tax, levying a separate estate tax. The following is from the Center on Budget and Policy Priorities:

> Fifteen states that levied pick-up taxes prior to 2001 retained estate taxes. Of these, twelve states—Delaware, Hawaii, Illinois, Maine, Maryland, Massachusetts, Minnesota, New Jersey, New York, North Carolina, Rhode Island, and Vermont—and the District of Columbia decoupled from the federal estate tax law and continue to levy an estate tax that is the same or very similar to the earlier pick-up tax. Three states—Connecticut, Oregon, and Washington—replaced their pick-up taxes with estate taxes that are not tied to the federal tax.[31]

Maintaining separate state and federal estate taxes is a significant divergence from past practice. When the modern version of the federal estate tax was first implemented in the early part of the 20th century (1916), the federal estate tax was somewhat controversial for state tax authorities. Up until that time, the taxation (or lack of taxation) of estates was viewed as a decision that should be left to the states.[32] A federal tax would, in theory, impinge on the states' capacity to raise revenue from a tax levied on wealth transfers at death.

These "historical precedence" claims by state officials, however, may have been overstated. The federal government has imposed temporary levies on the transfer of assets at death several times in the past. The revenue from these temporary levies was used to help pay for wars or national defense. The Stamp Act of 1797 was imposed on wills offered for probate and was repealed in 1802; the Revenue Act of 1862 imposed a similar stamp tax and an inheritance tax. Both were repealed in 1872. The War Revenue Act of 1898 created a so-called "legacy tax," which was levied on the estate and was the "precursor to the present federal estate tax."[33]

---

[30] U.S. Congress, Senate Committee on Finance, *Tax Reform: What It Means for State and Local Tax and Fiscal Policy*, 112th Cong., 2nd sess., Testimony of Walter Hellerstein, "Federal-State Tax Coordination: What Congress Should or Should Not Do," April 25, 2012.

[31] Elizabeth McNichol, *State Taxes on Inherited Wealth Remain Common: 22 States Levy an Estate or Inheritance Tax*, Center on Budget and Policy Priorities, January 4, 2012. Ohio's estate tax expires on January 1, 2013, and Delaware's July 1, 2013. The report is available at http://www.cbpp.org/cms/index.cfm?fa=view&id=337.

[32] U.S. Congress, Senate Committee on Finance, *Tax Reform: What It Means for State and Local Tax and Fiscal Policy*, 112th Cong., 2nd sess., Testimony of Walter Hellerstein, "Federal-State Tax Coordination: What Congress Should or Should Not Do," April 25, 2012.

[33] For more, see Jacobsen, Darien B., Brian G. Raub, and Barry W. Johnson, "The Estate Tax: Ninety Years and Counting," *Statistics of Income Bulletin*, 2007, p. 120.

Nevertheless, the federal government structured the initial federal estate tax such that any state tax would be credited dollar-for-dollar up to a specified tax rate on the estate. This provision created the equivalent of a revenue sharing arrangement between the federal government and the states as most states structured their taxes to match exactly the federal credit.[34] The state taxes "sponged up" any available credit. This degree of voluntary vertical coordination was unique to the estate tax.

This credit structure (pre-2001 law) had the advantage over the deduction structure (2012 law), from an economic and tax policy perspective, of virtually eliminating the incentive for states to "compete" among themselves to offer the lowest estate tax rates. If a state decided to levy an estate tax below the rates outlined for the federal credit, the decedent would simply pay more federal estate taxes. Thus, in addition to vertical coordination, horizontal coordination, as described earlier, would be strongly supported by this approach.

As outlined above, the overall simplicity of the estate tax is diminished if states and the federal government do not coordinate. For example, taxpayers, or their estates, would need to establish the location and taxability of assets, and both the federal and state governments would need to verify these claims. With a patchwork of state estate taxes and rules governing asset location, this process would be complicated. Over time, taxpayers would likely develop tax minimization strategies, further increasing compliance costs and complicating administrative oversight of the estate tax.

Equity

The equity (or "fairness") of a tax can be measured both vertically and horizontally. Vertical equity is evaluated by comparing the tax burden across individuals with different abilities to pay. Horizontal equity is evaluated by comparing the tax burden of individuals in otherwise similar economic circumstances. For an estate tax, a vertically equitable progressive estate tax would collect a larger share of the underlying estate as the value of the estate increases. A horizontally equitable estate tax would treat like-situated individuals (or decedents) in a like manner.

The estate tax is considered highly progressive with the "top ten percent of income earners paying virtually all of the tax; over half is paid by the richest 1 in 1,000."[35] State estate taxes are also progressive, though the burden is not as concentrated in the top wealth brackets. Most state estate taxes had lower exemption amounts, which means more taxable estates. State estate tax rates are lower than federal rates, thus there are more taxable estates at the state level, but the average state tax paid is less than the federal estate tax paid.

Assessing the federal and state taxes together, the deduction for state estate taxes (2012 law), rather than the credit (pre-2001 law), has some impact on the vertical equity. The deduction treatment makes the tax slightly less progressive, as the deduction is worth more to estates in the higher marginal tax brackets. Reversion to the pre-2001 law and the return of the credit for state death taxes, however, would not make the estate tax more progressive when compared with the President's budget proposal or extension of the 2012 law. The reason is that the other parameters

---

[34] The state death tax credit was enacted in 1924. For more history of the estate tax, see Jacobsen, Darien B., Brian G. Raub, and Barry W. Johnson, "The Estate Tax: Ninety Years and Counting," *Statistics of Income Bulletin*, 2007.

[35] Urban-Brookings Tax Policy Center, "Wealth Transfer Taxes," *The Tax Policy Briefing Book*, available at http://www.taxpolicycenter.org/upload/Elements/II-9KEYELEMENTS_WealthTransferTaxes.final.pdf.

of the pre-2001 federal estate tax included a lower exemption amount, capturing many more smaller estates, and do not provide for spousal portability of the exemption. The higher top rate in pre-2001 law, set at 55%, would regain some progressivity, but overall, the pre-2001 law is less progressive than the President's budget proposal.

Horizontal equity is achieved if taxpayers in equal positions are taxed in equal amounts. For an estate tax, estates of like size should be taxed in like manner. There is some debate concerning how to define "like" estates. Using only total value of assets may not be considered fair, as some estates have less liquid assets. These estates, usually with a significant share of business assets, may be constrained in their ability to pay the estate tax. Special provisions exist for farms and small businesses to allow them to pay the tax in installments over a maximum of 10 years.[36] These special provisions add complexity while potentially reducing compliance costs for liquidity-constrained entities.

Economic Efficiency

Efficient taxes are those that have a minimal impact on the behavior of taxpayers. Estate taxes can be identified as an inefficient tax for two principle reasons. One, the estate tax influences the investment decisions of taxpayers. If investments are taxed at death, then taxpayers will, in theory, invest less. Alternatively, if taxpayers have in mind a targeted value of assets to transfer at death, a tax that reduces the value of assets would mean more would have to be saved to achieve that target value. Either outcome would generate a loss in economic efficiency as decisions are made based on tax consequences, not underlying economic merit.

Taxpayers also devote considerable resources to minimizing estate tax liability. These costs are non-pecuniary, such as those distortions described above, as well as direct. The direct cost includes the fees paid to lawyers and accountants to plan any avoidance strategies.[37]

Of the three options explored here, the different tax rates and exemption levels would determine the size of the efficiency loss. The higher rates and lower exemption amounts that would accompany return to the pre-2001 law would likely generate the greatest changes in taxpayer behavior. Thus, return to pre-2001 law would generate the greatest economic efficiency loss (or deadweight loss). However, reinstating the credit for state death taxes instead of the deduction would mitigate this efficiency loss. In contrast, a deduction for state estate taxes, which would accompany both extension of the 2012 law and the Administration's budget proposal based on 2009 law, increases the tax burden and thus the economic efficiency loss arising from state estate taxes. The direct costs would also be greater with a deduction for state estate taxes because variation among states would present more avoidance opportunities and planning strategies.

Some have suggested that state estate taxes influence retirement residency choices. In theory, a state with relatively low estate taxes (or taxes generally) would be more attractive to wealthy retirees seeking to avoid taxes.[38] The perception that a state provides a more favorable tax

---

[36] 26 U.S.C § 6166.

[37] For and extensive discussion of avoidance behaviors in the pre-2001 law, see Richard Schmalbeck, "Avoiding Federal Wealth Transfer Taxes," in Gale, William G., James R. Hines Jr., Joel Slemrod, eds., *Rethinking Estate and Gift Taxation*, Brookings Institution Press, Washington, D.C., 2001, pp. 113-163.

[38] This theory, however, has not been confirmed empirically. For more, see Conway, Karen Smith and Jonathan C. Rork, "State 'Death' Taxes and Elderly Migration Revisited," *State Tax Notes*, June 6, 2006, pp. 785-789.

environment for retirees (or those close to death) may be enough to induce relocations based only on tax effect. Moves induced by tax preferences alone generate inefficiencies. A tax credit for state estate taxes could virtually eliminate the incentive to move, as the state tax would not add an additional state tax burden.

Revenue Sufficiency

A final criteria is whether the tax raises enough revenue, or prevents the loss of revenue from other tax sources, to justify its imposition. This section presents data for federal and state estate taxes from two different sources, the Internal Revenue Service (IRS) and the U.S. Census Bureau (CB). The IRS data report federal estate and gift tax collections by state and the CB data report state estate, gift, and inheritance tax collections. The two sets of data are compared to exhibit how revenue from the estate tax for each level of government has changed from pre-EGTRRA laws (2001) to post-EGTRRA laws (2009) for each state.[39]

In 2001, estates generated significant revenue for both state and the federal governments. For 2001, just over $31 billion was collected, with the states collecting $7.5 billion and the federal government collecting $23.5 billion (see **Table 4**). By 2009, estate and gift tax collections had declined to $25.3 billion, with the federal government collecting $20.6 billion (a 12.3% decline) and state governments collecting a combined $4.7 billion (a 37.9% decline). The decline is even more severe if the 2001 data are adjusted for inflation. Converting the 2001 data into 2009 dollars yields total revenue of $37.5 billion with state collections at $9.1 billion and federal collections of $28.5 billion (see **Figure 1**).

The decline has at least two possible sources, tax policy changes and the recession from December 2007 through June 2009. It is likely that almost all the 2009 federal estate tax filings were for deaths that occurred during the recession. However, the 2001 data likely include a significant number of deaths that occurred during the 2001 recession, which spanned from March through November of that year. Assets such as stock holdings, personal residences, and other real estate holdings accounted for 41.8% of taxable estate value in 2009.[40] Those same assets accounted for more taxable estate value in 2001 (51.6%). The change in value can be explained almost entirely by the change in the value of stock in decedent portfolios, which dropped from 36.0% in 2001 to 25.4% in 2009. The drop in the value of stock as a portion of the decedent portfolio is also explained by the increased exemption amount eliminating estates at the lower end of the distribution. The average estate subject to federal estate taxes was larger in 2009, reflecting the elimination of the smaller estates. Stock holdings as a share of decedent portfolio rise with the size of the estate. Thus, if the average estate size is larger in 2009, then the concentration of publicly traded stock is more important.

As noted earlier, the Economic Growth and Tax Relief Reconciliation Act of 2001 (EGTRRA) phased out the credit in stages and replaced it with a deduction. The Tax Relief, Unemployment Insurance Reauthorization, and Job Creation Act of 2010 (TRUIRJCA) extended the deduction

---

[39] The IRS data are for the filing year and the CB data are for the state fiscal year. Summing the two does present some concern particularly for 2009. In 2009, the IRS data likely reflect mostly information from deaths occurring in calendar year 2008 under 2008 tax laws. The CB data are revenues from estate and gift taxes collected between July 1, 2008, and June 30, 2009. The CB data likely include data from deaths that occurred in 2007 under 2007 tax law.

[40] CRS Report RS20593, *Asset Distribution of Taxable Estates: An Analysis*, by Steven Maguire.

---

structure through 2012. In 2013, the credit along with higher rates and lower exemption amounts are set to return.

Concluding Observations

Each of the proposals identified here offers a mixed bag of economic effects. Reverting to the pre-2001 law as scheduled would likely increase intergovernmental coordination and reduce compliance costs for medium to larger estates. The pre-2001 law, however, would capture more estates with the lower exemption amount of $1 million. These smaller estates would encounter compliance costs with reversion to pre-2001 law, as they would not be subject to estate taxes under the other two proposals. The added compliance costs of these smaller estates would counter the reduced compliance cost of the larger estates with the reintroduction of the credit for state death taxes.

The equity and the efficiency of a tax often work against each other. Achieving greater equity often comes with the cost of reduced efficiency. Further complicating the analysis is the perception or definition of equity, which is somewhat subjective. Generally, reversion to pre-2001 law would reduce the progressivity (compared with the 2012 law and the FY2013 budget proposal) of the federal estate tax as more, smaller estates would be subject to the tax.[41] The federal tax code more generally, however, would become more progressive, as tax burdens on the relatively wealthy would increase. There is not a clear measure to identify the more equitable policy.

The estate tax impacts the economy more broadly as saving and capital investment become less attractive the higher the tax. In theory, lower estate tax burdens encourage more saving and investment. The higher exemption amounts and lower rates offered by the 2012 law and the FY2013 budget proposal would be preferred using this one-dimensional criteria. The lower tax burden, while theoretically encouraging more investment, necessarily reduces the revenue yield of the estate tax.

Which course of action Congress will choose is uncertain and the impact on the states unclear. Coordination with states would likely reduce administrative and compliance costs of the estate tax, increase the progressivity of the code generally, and possibly increase the economic efficiency of state estate taxes.

---

[41] In theory, the estate tax should be a progressive tax. The "optimal" level of progressivity in the estate tax, however, is uncertain. See the following for more: Farhi, Emmanuel and Ivan Werning, "Progressive Estate Taxation," *Quarterly Journal of Economics*, May 2010, pp. 635-673.

Table 4. Federal and State Estate Tax Revenues, by State, 2001 and 2009

Dollar Amounts in 000s

State of Residence	2001				2009			
	State	Fed	Total	State Share	State	Fed	Total	State Share
Total	$7,499,439	$23,531,334	$31,030,773	24.2%	$4,654,053	$20,643,664	$25,297,717	18.4%
Alabama	47,261	267,381	314,642	15.0%	-	177,599	177,599	0.0%
Alaska	2,683	35,854	38,537	7.0%	175	17,154	17,329	1.0%
Arizona	76,922	264,485	341,407	22.5%	210	628,316	628,526	0.0%
Arkansas	26,101	118,192	144,293	18.1%	224	81,427	81,651	0.3%
California	934,708	4,000,821	4,935,529	18.9%	245	4,447,354	4,447,599	0.0%
Colorado	82,798	276,209	359,007	23.1%	22	226,344	226,366	0.0%
Connecticut	257,801	449,764	707,565	36.4%	230,503	530,825	761,328	30.3%
Delaware	41,037	78,147	119,184	34.4%	-	73,527	73,527	0.0%
District of Columbia	45,670	235,788	281,458	16.2%	74,508	71,504	146,012	51.0%
Florida	707,565	2,521,963	3,229,528	21.9%	4,800	2,712,161	2,716,961	0.2%
Georgia	126,114	498,740	624,854	20.2%	83	330,248	330,331	0.0%
Hawaii	17,541	31,390	48,931	35.8%	274	96,490	96,764	0.3%
Idaho	42,808	55,393	98,201	43.6%	264	118,333	118,597	0.2%
Illinois	361,039	1,202,226	1,563,265	23.1%	287,757	780,250	1,068,007	26.9%
Indiana	163,674	392,172	555,846	29.4%	185,662	196,117	381,779	48.6%
Iowa	87,670	120,984	208,654	42.0%	72,562	95,098	167,660	43.3%
Kansas	41,195	123,672	164,867	25.0%	22,530	134,138	156,668	14.4%
Kentucky	85,160	194,981	280,141	30.4%	41,234	120,297	161,531	25.5%
Louisiana	82,930	107,960	190,890	43.4%	5,068	286,314	291,382	1.7%
Maine	30,616	120,917	151,533	20.2%	31,819	59,868	91,687	34.7%
Maryland	168,751	435,990	604,741	27.9%	205,627	251,588	457,215	45.0%
Massachusetts	203,381	666,922	870,303	23.4%	259,734	441,458	701,192	37.0%

The Impact of the Federal Estate Tax on State Estate Taxes

State of Residence	2001				2009			
	State	Fed	Total	State Share	State	Fed	Total	State Share
Michigan	155,469	606,645	762,114	20.4%	147	222,530	222,677	0.1%
Minnesota	53,377	113,507	166,884	32.0%	129,811	197,229	327,040	39.7%
Mississippi	27,575	108,733	136,308	20.2%	-	79,922	79,922	0.0%
Missouri	153,689	526,504	680,193	22.6%	3,030	555,025	558,055	0.5%
Montana	20,286	57,425	77,711	26.1%	213	59,929	60,142	0.4%
Nebraska	27,411	95,727	123,138	22.3%	493	85,702	86,195	0.6%
Nevada	39,918	167,196	207,114	19.3%	-	120,536	120,536	0.0%
New Hampshire	59,266	117,354	176,620	33.6%	77	101,346	101,423	0.1%
New Jersey	478,061	969,865	1,447,926	33.0%	639,544	514,053	1,153,597	55.4%
New Mexico	23,261	84,221	107,482	21.6%	32	68,263	68,295	0.0%
New York	758,523	2,124,843	2,883,366	26.3%	1,165,247	1,956,392	3,121,639	37.3%
North Carolina	143,419	447,392	590,811	24.3%	116,624	237,410	354,034	32.9%
North Dakota	5,056	7,861	12,917	39.1%	40	17,333	17,373	0.2%
Ohio	166,004	900,794	1,066,798	15.6%	64,403	434,588	498,991	12.9%
Oklahoma	84,806	239,356	324,162	26.2%	39,562	147,568	187,130	21.1%
Oregon	42,077	184,325	226,402	18.6%	87,211	129,394	216,605	40.3%
Pennsylvania	776,869	1,060,935	1,837,804	42.3%	748,648	623,711	1,372,359	54.6%
Rhode Island	27,320	89,369	116,689	23.4%	27,262	26,819	54,081	50.4%
South Carolina	49,488	222,519	272,007	18.2%	153	186,779	186,932	0.1%
South Dakota	34,925	41,857	76,782	45.5%	16	27,462	27,478	0.1%
Tennessee	84,140	361,213	445,353	18.9%	91,490	164,499	255,989	35.7%
Texas	322,355	1,170,785	1,493,140	21.6%	2,004	1,411,624	1,413,628	0.1%
Utah	30,017	71,181	101,198	29.7%	321	47,559	47,880	0.7%
Vermont	12,714	33,544	46,258	27.5%	23,397	16,847	40,244	58.1%
Virginia	126,839	593,730	720,569	17.6%	6,005	534,547	540,552	1.1%

The Impact of the Federal Estate Tax on State Estate Taxes

State of Residence	2001				2009			
	State	Fed	Total	State Share	State	Fed	Total	State Share
Washington	106,311	422,227	528,538	20.1%	138,535	356,326	494,861	28.0%
West Virginia	17,541	37,849	55,390	31.7%	29	17,153	17,182	0.2%
Wisconsin	77,084	278,881	355,965	21.7%	20,853	272,134	292,987	7.1%
Wyoming	7,883	69,735	77,618	10.2%	113	49,379	49,492	0.2%

Source: State tax revenue data are from the U.S. Census Bureau and federal tax revenue data are from the U.S. Internal Revenue Service.

Notes: The state tax revenue data are for the fiscal year. The federal tax revenue data are for the calendar filing year. Thus, the tax revenue are not from the same estates.

Table 5. Federal Estate Tax Rate Schedule, Pre-2001 Changes

Taxable Estate Value From	to	Current Statutory Rate (in Percent)
$0	$10,000	18
$10,001	$20,000	20
$20,001	$40,000	22
$40,001	$60,000	24
$60,001	$80,000	26
$80,001	$100,000	28
$100,001	$150,000	30
$150,001	$250,000	32
$250,001	$500,000	34
$500,001	$750,000	37
$750,001	$1,000,000	39
$1,000,001	$1,250,000	41
$1,250,001	$1,500,000	43
$1,500,001	$2,000,000	45
$2,000,001	$2,500,000	49
$2,500,001	$3,000,000	53
$3,000,001	and over	55

Source: Federal Tax Code.

Table 6. Federal Credit for State Death Taxes Schedule

In 2012, the Amount is Claimed as Deduction when Calculating Federal Estate Tax Liability

Taxable Estate Value (less the $60,000 exemption)	to	Current Statutory Credit Rate (in Percent)
$0	$40,000	0
$40,001	$90,000	.8
$90,001	$140,000	1.6
$140,001	$240,000	2.4
$240,001	$440,000	3.2
$440,001	$640,000	4.0
$640,001	$840,000	4.8
$840,001	$1,040,000	5.6
$1,040,001	$1,540,000	6.4
$1,540,001	$2,040,000	7.2

Taxable Estate Value (less the $60,000 exemption)	to	Current Statutory Credit Rate (in Percent)
$2,040,001	$2,540,000	8.0
$2,540,001	$3,040,000	8.8
$3,040,001	$3,540,000	9.6
$3,540,001	$4,040,000	10.4
$4,040,001	$5,040,000	11.2
$5,040,001	$6,040,000	12.0
$6,040,001	$7,040,000	12.8
$7,040,001	$8,040,000	13.6
$8,040,001	$9,040,000	14.4
$9,040,001	$10,040,000	15.2
$10,040,001	and over	16.0

Source: Federal Tax Code.

Author Contact Information

Steven Maguire
Specialist in Public Finance
smaguire@crs.loc.gov, 7-7841

www.ingramcontent.com/pod-product-compliance
Lightning Source LLC
Chambersburg PA
CBHW081307170526
45165CB00010B/3288